BERRIES

A COOKBOOK

BY ROBERT BERKLEY • PHOTOGRAPHS BY ERIC JACOBSON

CASSELL

A RUNNING HEADS BOOK

Copyright © 1990
by Running Heads Incorporated.

First published in U.K. by Cassell Publishers 1990.

Cassell Publishers Limited
Artillery House, Artillery Row
London SW1P 1RT

BERRIES: A COOKBOOK
was produced and conceived by
Running Heads Incorporated
55 West 21st Street
New York, New York 10010

Senior Editor: Sarah Kirshner
Designer: Lesley Ehlers
Production Manager: Linda Winters
Managing Editor: Lindsey Crittenden

10   9   8   7   6   5   4   3   2   1

British Library Cataloging in Publication Data

Berkley, Robert.
  Berries.
  1. Food. Dishes using berries. Recipes.
  I. Title.
  641.6'47
  ISBN 0-304-31934-1

Typeset by Trufont Typographers, Inc.
Color Separations by Hong Kong Scanner Craft Company, Ltd.
Printed and bound in Singapore by Times Offset Pte Ltd.

To my mother, my grandparents and Michelle.

Special thanks to Mary Trasko, Mildred Raucher and Mary Forsell for
their contributions of materials for this book. Thanks to Michelle Hauser,
Nancy and Sam Freitag, Loretta and Bruno Hauser, Kate Struby, Meggin
Siefert, Robin Page, Maggie Jones, Judy Devine, Myriam Zwierzinska,
Doug Hay, Rick Silverness, Jennifer Barnaby, prop stylist, and Brendan
Mullany, photo assistant. Thanks to Marta Hallett, Ellen Milionis, Sarah
Kirshner, Lindsey Crittenden and all the other support at Running Heads.

Thanks to the following for their generosity: ABC Bed Bath and Linens;
Marek Cecula, designer, and Pascal Golay, designer; Contemporary
Porcelain; Gear Stores; Bill Goldsmith, plate designer; Marble Connection;
Umbrello.

CONTENTS

INTRODUCTION

When I think of berries, the first thing that comes to mind is a sensation I experienced as a teenager. I was driving through central North Carolina with a friend on a sunny late morning in June. We were driving on a state highway when we found ourselves along a series of mountains, and decided to stop the car by the base of one of the mountains to hike.

Since there were no paths through the thickets, we had to create one. After a long climb we rested, and while catching our breath from the heat and the strenuous hike, we noticed a blackberry bush. We each dared the other to try a berry; one of us finally did, and when he didn't keel over from poison, and found that it was good, we managed to devour almost every berry on that bush.

Every time I eat a really fresh berry, I recall the combination of the sun, the fresh air, the mountains of North Carolina, being sixteen and the supreme sensual experience of the slightly sour berry juice bursting between my teeth. Even the word berries is enough to evoke the abundance of all these sensations.

It took me a long time and certain prejudices to overcome before I began cooking with berries; I didn't want to spoil their organic intensity. After all, cooking is by definition a process of destruction: breaking down fibres, altering flavours, changing forms. How could a fresh berry be improved? Cooking with berries demands different expectations and requires a different approach. Within each berry lies a multitude of different flavours and textures which can be drawn out to do whatever you as a cook want them to do. Depending on the demands of a dish, the elements within a berry can be used to thicken sauce, change colour, balance spiciness, counteract bitterness—all while lending to the dish the distinct and sublime character of the particular berry. The idea of drawing out more savoury and fuller, rounder flavours from a berry can be a very exciting challenge to an inquisitive cook.

The recipes in this book are designed to illustrate the diversity of cooking with berries. In some cases simply adding a fresh berry to an assortment of ingredients is all that is required, the pristine state of the berry speaking for itself within the arrangement of the dish. In other cases we put the berry through various cooking stages to elicit the different degrees of character in each berry. In fact almost entire identities change in different cooking processes.

For example, in comparing Blueberry Vichyssoise with Blueberry Pie, it's hard to believe the same ingredient is used in both dishes. The different tastes of the same berry in reaction to the other ingredients—one earthy, potatoey, the other syrupy, fruity and sweet—demonstrates two parts of the spectrum of this wide-ranging fruit.

Another striking example is what can happen to a soup when we substitute berries for other ingredients. Gazpacho calls for tartness. Usually a little vinegar or lemon juice fills that vacancy and gently supports the other ingredients—tomato, cucumbers, peppers—so that the focus of attention is on them, while the lemon or vinegar acts as a sort of post, quietly holding up the structure. In Cranberry Gazpacho, the cranberry is gentle enough not to overshadow everything else but intense enough to be the dominant flavour of the soup, with the other ingredients acting in support of it—an exciting variation on a traditional dish.

In a similar vein, I have chosen closely related recipes that share certain procedures and ingredients but use different berries. In Smoked Trout and Raspberry Salad with Lingonberry Dressing, raspberries are used for their soft flavour. A more sour berry would certainly work well with the bitter flavour of the rocket, but would confound the saltiness of the smoked fish. In the Bitter Greens Salad with Strawberries and Gooseberry Vinaigrette, strawberries are used so as not to detract from the sharpness of the goat's cheese. The common element in both salads is the bitter flavour of the greens. Both berries work comfortably with their other accompaniments—the smoked trout and the cheese—and these accompaniments work equally well with the greens. What becomes interesting is the flavours that become apparent in the *greens* when combined with the *berries*. The bitterness seems to change when introduced to the exceptionally subtle differences in the two berries. The recipes illustrate the range of character of each berry and its capacity to work well with other ingredients in a way that a straight taste test between a strawberry and a raspberry could not.

The fragility of flavour that makes berries so desirable isn't always easy to obtain. You can't always be on a Carolina mountainside when blackberries reach their height of perfection. As with many other types of produce, different berries are in season at different times and do not grow for much of the rest of the year, nor do they grow in the most accessible places. Blueberries are in season from July through August, as are currants. Blackberries are available from August through September. Cranberries are in season from early November through mid-February. Strawberries are in season from May through October, and raspberries are available June through October. But many berries are now available year-round. It is rare to experience a really fresh cloudberry at any time outside Scandinavia. Although modern shipping techniques can provide people all over the world with berries from other places, between the time delays of harvest and sorting, shipping and distributing, several days may have passed by the time a person goes to market for these berries. And although well-travelled berries remain fresh, they cannot provide a quintessential tasting experience. Shopping at reputable greengrocers should ensure freshness and quality.

When shopping for fresh berries, the main things to avoid are mould (fuzzy whiteness on the undersides of the berries) and softness. A little bit of mould is all right, but it spreads quickly. A berry is probably soft if it looks wrinkled or deflated. Mouldy berries aren't good for cooking or eating. Soft berries, however, can be used for preserves or pies with no loss of flavor.

Generations of cooks have developed storage techniques that enable people to enjoy late-summer and spring berries in the middle of winter. Freezing is the most obvious method. Sealed airtight in a rigid plastic container or wrapped snugly in freezer film, berries will keep for up to four or five months in the freezer.

Drying is a natural means of preserving the essence of a berry. In the same way that a raisin is a dehydrated form of a grape, dried berries retain much of their original berry essence. Delicatessens and speciality food shops sometimes carry varieties of sun-dried berries—well worth looking for. They can be stored at room temperature, in a cupboard or in a paper bag for months and months with no loss of sweetness or flavour. For several recipes in this book—Dried Berry Bagels, for example—dried berries are used to a greater advantage than their fresh equivalent. The bagels undergo a wet cooking stage followed by a dry cooking stage. Dried berries maintain their form and withstand the drastic change in cooking techniques where the fresh varieties would lose their own moisture during the wet stage and bleed during the dry stage.

Wines, juices, brandies and vinegars also capture the essence of a berry in an extremely subtle way when used reservedly. The presence of a blueberry vinegar mixed with olive oil in a salad dressing can suggest aromatically the presence of a blueberry. The same blueberry vinegar can be reduced in a pan and enriched with butter to make a creamy sauce for fish. Depending on the vehicle—olive oil or butter—and the final subject of the dish—salad or fish—you can experience the essence of blueberry in two vastly different ways.

Perhaps my favourite means of saving berries is through preserves. Preserving melts the membranes that hold a berry together, breaks down the fine fibres that keep it from simply turning into juice and, through a long and slow cooking process, transforms a bunch of whole berries into something almost completely different. It is through this process that many interactions occur. Although a recipe for preserves is a simple series of steps, it is perhaps one of the most complex chemical exchanges of berry cooking. The membranes themselves seem to dissolve in the pan and evaporate with all the steam, but they remain, helping to thicken and preserve the berries.

The uses of preserves are as diverse and plentiful as the fresh berries themselves. When added to a reduced stock, they give it body and turn it into a sauce. When added to softened butter with egg yolk and caster sugar, they make the ultimate cake icing. When added to soured cream they make a delicately balanced salad dressing. Or they can be enjoyed simply with sweet butter spread on good bread. For me, tasting well-made preserves is like being in the centre of a berry.

For the most part, each recipe in this book—as is the case with most recipes—should be viewed as a blueprint to a dish, a guideline to use as a point of reference. Many of the berries are interchangeable. The 'lumpy' berries—raspberries, blackberries, loganberries, mulberries—are natural substitutes for one another in shape as well as taste, as are the 'smooth' berries—blueberries, cranberries, red- and blackcurrants, lingonberries, gooseberries and rosehips. These are not hard and fast categories for substitutions, just suggestions. Regional, less common berries fall into these categories as well. Try using raspberries or strawberries for cranberries and you'll become familiar with the enormous range of possibilities within the berry family. This explorative approach can be applied to other groups of ingredients as well, adding an entire new dimension to your cooking repertoire.

DRIED BERRY BAGELS

7 g (¼ oz) dried yeast
1 tablespoon caster sugar
250 ml (8 fl oz) warm water
    (about 43°C/110°F)
560 g (1¼ lb) strong plain flour
1 teaspoon salt
2 eggs
2 tablespoons vegetable oil
35 g (1¼ oz) dried blueberries
35 g (1¼ oz) dried cranberries
2 tablespoons water
1 egg yolk
(Note: dried blackcurrants may
    be substituted for dried
    berries)

· Preheat oven to 190°C (375°F
  or gas 5).
· In a bowl, place yeast, sugar
  and warm water. Allow to
  stand for 5 minutes. Yeast will
  foam. If the water is too hot or
  too cold the yeast will not
  foam and the process must be
  repeated.
· Add 140 g (5 oz) of flour, salt
  and the 2 eggs to the mixture.
  Whisk together to incorporate
  flour.
· Gradually add the remaining
  flour. Incorporate it with your
  fingers. Continue to add flour
  until the dough loses its stick-
  iness. Knead the dough for 5
  minutes. This will activate the
  protein in the flour to make it
  rise, and give it elasticity.
· Coat a large bowl with half the
  vegetable oil. Place dough in
  the bowl and cover with a
  damp cloth. Leave it to rise at
  room temperature for about 30
  minutes.
· Cut dough into 14 equal pieces
  and allow to rise for another
  20 minutes. Work the dried
  berries into the dough pieces.
· With your finger, poke a hole
  in the centre of each piece, and
  form into the shape of a bagel.
· Heat a large pan of unsalted
  water to boiling. Lower to a
  simmer. Place the bagels in the
  simmering water for 3–4 minutes. Turn over and simmer for
  another 3–4 minutes.
· Coat a large baking tin with
  the remaining vegetable oil.
· Beat 2 tablespoons of water
  with the egg yolk. Brush each
  bagel with the egg wash and
  place in the baking tin.
· Bake for about 35 minutes or
  until golden brown.

Makes 14 bagels.
Preparation time: 2½ hours.

BLACKCURRANT
CRÊPES

2 eggs
100 g (3½ oz) caster sugar
2 tablespoons plain flour
120 ml (4 fl oz) milk
90 g (3 oz) fresh blackcurrants
60 g (2 oz) unsalted butter
125 g (4 oz) ricotta cheese

· In a bowl, combine eggs, half
 of the sugar and flour. Add the
 milk. For thinner crêpes, add
 more milk. Allow to stand for
 1 hour.
· In a 2 litre (3½ pint) saucepan,
 simmer the blackcurrants, just
 covered with water and remaining sugar. Cook for about
 2 minutes. Remove from the
 water, drain and allow to cool.
· In a 15 cm (6 inch) non-stick

frying pan, melt ½ teaspoon
butter. When the butter begins
to crackle, add 2 tablespoons
of the crêpe batter, enough to
evenly cover the pan. When it
forms a solid coating on the
bottom, after about 1 minute,
flip it. Continue cooking for a
few seconds, and slide on to a
large clean surface. Allow to
cool. Repeat until all of batter
is used.
· Spoon about 2 tablespoons of
 the ricotta cheese along the
 centre of each crêpe.
· Spoon about 2 tablespoons of
 the blackcurrants directly
 alongside the cheese. Roll each
 crêpe to form a log.

Serves 8–10.
Preparation time: 1¼ hours.

RASPBERRY PRESERVE

500 g (1 lb) fresh raspberries
200 g (7 oz) sugar
1 litre (1¾ pints) cold water
skins from 2 Granny Smith
  apples, tied securely in
  muslin

· In a 4 litre (7 pint) preserving
  pan (copper preferred), heat all
  ingredients to the boil, stirring
  often.
· Reduce heat to the lowest
possible heat and cook for 6
hours, or until mixture is firm,
stirring frequently. Add more
water gradually, if necessary.
· Cool, uncovered, in refrigerator. When completely cool,
  cover with polythene or pot in
  a seal-tight glass jar. Can keep
  up to several months.

Makes 500–750 ml (¾–1¼
pints) preserve.
Preparation time: 10 hours.

AMERICAN-STYLE PECAN MUFFINS WITH MULBERRIES

100 g (3½ oz) ground pecans
70 g (2½ oz) plain flour
2 tablespoons baking powder
50 g (scant 2 oz) caster sugar
1 egg
30 g (1 oz) unsalted butter,
    melted and cooled
120 ml (4 fl oz) warm milk
1 teaspoon vanilla essence
pinch of salt
70 g (2½ oz) dried mulberries,
    or any dried berries

· Preheat oven to 180°C (350°F
  or gas 4).
· Combine pecans, flour, baking
  powder and sugar. Add egg,
  butter, milk, vanilla essence,
  salt and mulberries. Allow to
  stand for 10 minutes.
· Fill 4 cups of a non-stick deep
  bun tray with the mixture.
· Bake for 8–10 minutes, or until
  a skewer inserted in the centre
  of a muffin comes out clean.

Serves 4.
Preparation time: 30 minutes.

AMERICAN-STYLE CORNMEAL MUFFINS WITH MULBERRIES AND POPPYSEEDS

60 g (2 oz) cornmeal
70 g (2½ oz) plain flour
2 tablespoons baking powder
50 g (scant 2 oz) caster sugar
1 egg
30 g (1 oz) unsalted butter,
    melted and cooled
70 g (2½ oz) dried mulberries,
    or any dried berries
90 g (3 oz) black poppyseeds
120 ml (4 fl oz) warm milk
pinch of salt
1 teaspoon vanilla essence
grated zest of 1 lemon

· Preheat oven to 180°C (350°F
  or gas 4).
· Combine cornmeal, flour, baking powder and sugar. Add
  egg, butter and mulberries.
· In a separate bowl, soak
  poppy-seeds in milk for 5
  minutes. Add both ingredients
  to the mixture.
· Add salt, vanilla essence and
  lemon zest. Allow to stand for
  10 minutes.
· Fill 4 cups of a non-stick deep
  bun tin with the mixture.
· Bake for about 8–10 minutes,
  or until a skewer comes out
  clean when you poke it
  through the centre of a muffin.

Serves 4.
Preparation time: 30 minutes.

BLUEBERRY CORNMEAL GRIDDLE CAKES

125 g (4 oz) cornmeal
1 teaspoon salt
2 tablespoons honey
250 ml (8 fl oz) boiling water
1 egg
120 ml (4 fl oz) milk
30 g (1 oz) unsalted butter, melted
70 g (2½ oz) plain flour
2 tablespoons baking powder
75 g (2½ oz) blueberries
30 g (1 oz) unsalted butter

· In a bowl, combine cornmeal, salt, honey and boiling water. Mix until smooth. Let cool slightly.
· Add the egg, milk and melted butter to the cornmeal mixture.
· Sift in the flour and baking powder. Add the blueberries.
· Set aside for 10 minutes.
· Melt 15 g (½ oz) butter in a large heavy frying pan over medium-high heat.
· Pour 4 tablespoons batter into pan for each griddle cake, well spaced apart. When bubbles pop around the edges, and begin to form in the centre of each griddle cake, flip and cook for another minute. Serve hot, and make remaining griddle cakes in the same way.

Serves 4.
Preparation time: 30 minutes.

BLACKBERRY SYRUP

150 g (5 oz) fresh blackberries
350 ml (12 fl oz) water
1 whole cinnamon stick
85 g (3 oz) molasses
40 g (scant 1½ oz) light brown sugar
1 teaspoon vanilla essence

· Place blackberries, water and cinnamon stick in a small heavy saucepan, and cook over a low heat for about 20 minutes. Remove cinnamon stick and strain.
· Add molasses, sugar and vanilla essence. Allow to cool.

Makes 250 ml (8 fl oz).
Preparation time: 40 minutes.

GOLDEN RASPBERRY CRUMBCAKE

15 g (½ oz) unsalted butter
120 g (4 oz), plus 2 tablespoons
    plain flour
1 tablespoon baking powder
½ teaspoon salt
150 g (5 oz) caster sugar
60 g (2 oz) unsalted butter,
    melted and cooled
2 tablespoons vanilla essence
2 eggs
250 g (8 oz) golden raspberries
120 ml soured cream

CRUMB TOPPING:

125 g (4 oz) light brown sugar
125 g (4 oz) unsalted butter, cut
    into small pieces
210 g (7½ oz) plain flour

- Preheat oven to 180°C (350°F or gas 4).
- With 15 g (½ oz) butter, evenly grease a 22.5 × 17.5 cm (9 × 7 inch) baking tin.
- Dust with 2 tablespoons flour. Shake out excess. Refrigerate.
- In large bowl, combine remaining flour, baking powder, salt and sugar.
- Add the melted butter, vanilla essence and eggs. Mix until well combined.
- Fold in the raspberries and soured cream.
- Pour mixture into baking tin. Allow to stand for 10 minutes.
- In a separate bowl, combine brown sugar and butter pieces.
- Add flour and mix until evenly incorporated.
- Sprinkle evenly over cake mixture. Bake for 30 minutes or until a skewer inserted in the centre comes out clean.

Serves 6.
Preparation time: 45 minutes.

BLUEBERRY VICHYSSOISE

5 new potatoes, washed in cold
  water
4–5 spring onions, white part
  only
750 ml (1¼ pints) chicken stock
  (See below)
120 ml (4 fl oz) soured cream
150 g (5 oz) blueberries
120 ml (4 fl oz) milk

· Cut washed potatoes into
  quarters.
· Cut spring onions into 1 cm
  (½ inch) pieces.
· In a 4 litre (7 pint) pan, heat
  chicken stock, potatoes and
spring onions to the boil.
  Lower to a simmer.
· Cook for about 30 minutes,
  until potatoes are soft.
· Sieve stock mixture and return
  to pan; discard pulp left in
  sieve. Bring back to a simmer
  over a low heat.
· Whisk in the soured cream.
  Add ¾ of the berries and cook
  on low heat until the first
  berries split. Set aside remaining berries.
· Remove from heat and chill
  overnight.
· With a fork, mash the blueberry mixture and thin with
  the milk until desired consistency.
· Garnish with the remainder of
  the uncooked berries.

Serves 4.
Preparation time: 1½ hours,
plus overnight chilling.

CHICKEN STOCK

2 tablespoons vegetable oil
2 large carrots, thinly sliced
8–10 shallots, finely chopped
4 spring onions, finely chopped
1 Granny Smith apple, quartered with skins and seeds
15 g (½ oz) button mushrooms,
  coarsely chopped
500 g (1 lb) chicken wings
20–40 ice cubes
12–15 whole black peppercorns
2–3 cloves of garlic, crushed
1 bunch parsley

· Heat oil in a stockpot. When
  the oil is hot add the carrots,
  shallots, spring onions, apple
  and mushrooms. Cook for 10
  minutes.
· Add chicken wings, ice cubes,
  peppercorns and garlic.
· Cover all ingredients with cold
  water and top with parsley.
· Bring to the boil, and immediately lower to a simmer.
  Cook for about 2½–3 hours,
  skimming fat occasionally.
· Strain liquid, and discard vege-
  tables and wings.
· Keep chicken stock, covered,
  in refrigerator.

Makes 2–3 litres (3½–5 pints).
Preparation time: 4 hours.

CRANBERRY GAZPACHO

1 small cucumber
1 red pepper, cored and seeded
½ green pepper, cored and
    seeded
1 mild green chilli, seeded
2 large ripe tomatoes
4 spring onions
1 bunch parsley
1 tablespoon lemon juice or wine
    vinegar
salt and pepper
250 ml (8 fl oz) water
50 g (scant 2 oz) fresh
    cranberries

· Very finely chop cucumber,
  peppers, chilli, tomatoes,
  spring onions and parsley.

Combine in large bowl.
· Add lemon juice, salt and
  pepper. Set aside.
· In a 1 litre (2 pint) saucepan,
  bring the water to the boil.
  Cook cranberries for about 1
  minute, or until a few cranberries split. Allow the cranberries
  to cool. When cool, add them
  to the gazpacho.
· Cover and refrigerate
  overnight.

Serves 4.
Preparation time: 20 minutes,
plus overnight chilling.

CHILLED RASPBERRY
AND BLACKBERRY SOUP

45 g (1½ oz) red raspberries
50 g (scant 2 oz) blackberries
150 ml (¼ pint) buttermilk
150 ml (¼ pint) plain yogurt
pinch of salt

· Pass raspberries through a
  sieve and discard the seeds.
· In a separate bowl, pass blackberries through a sieve and
  discard the seeds.

· Add half the buttermilk and
  yogurt to the raspberry purée.
· Add half the buttermilk and
  yogurt to the blackberry purée.
· Add salt to each and chill for 1
  hour.
· With a 120 ml (4 fl oz) ladle
  pour the blackberry soup into
  each bowl; add a ladleful of the
  raspberry soup in the centre.

Serves 2.
Preparation time: 1 hour 20
minutes.

FIDDLEHEAD SALAD WITH BLUEBERRY VINAIGRETTE

VINAIGRETTE

4 tablespoons blueberry vinegar
1 tablespoon Dijon mustard
120–175 ml (4–6 fl oz) extra
   virgin olive oil
salt and pepper

500 g (1 lb) fresh fiddlehead
   ferns or sprue asparagus
1 red leaf lettuce
1 head radicchio
1 round lettuce
4 bunches mâche (corn salad)
150 g (5 oz) fresh blueberries

VINAIGRETTE:

· In a small bowl, whisk together the vinegar and the mustard. Add the olive oil, salt and pepper.

· Drop the fiddlehead ferns or asparagus into boiling water for 1 minute. Drain and refresh under cold water.
· Wash lettuce thoroughly in clean water.
· In a salad bowl, combine the salad leaves with the ferns or asparagus. Toss with the vinaigrette and garnish with the fresh blueberries.

Serves 16.
Preparation time: 20 minutes.

DRIED CRANBERRY COLE SLAW

150 g (5 oz) dried cranberries or
    dried blackcurrants
250 ml (8 fl oz) white zinfandel,
    or any blush or light rosé
    wine
250 ml (8 fl oz) vinaigrette (see
    page 34)
250 ml (8 fl oz) soured cream
250 ml (8 fl oz) mayonnaise
1 small red cabbage (about
    500 g/1 lb)
2 Spanish onions, thinly sliced
2–3 spring onions, thinly
    julienned
2 tablespoons ground cumin
60 g (2 oz) caster sugar
salt and pepper
Note: dried blackcurrants may
    be substituted for dried
    cranberries.

· Soak cranberries in wine overnight at room temperature.
· Combine vinaigrette, soured
  cream and mayonnaise. Set
  aside.
· Remove outer leaves from cabbage. Core and cut into quarters. Slice thinly.
· Combine onion and cabbage
  with soured cream mixture.
  Add the drained cranberries,
  spring onions, ground cumin,
  sugar and salt and pepper.
  Cover and refrigerate
  overnight.

Serves 10–12.
Preparation time: 20 minutes,
plus overnight twice.

CHICKEN SALAD
WITH BLACKBERRIES

1 chicken, about 1.75 kg (3½ lb)
salt and pepper
250 ml (8 fl oz) water
1 egg yolk
1 tablespoon Dijon mustard
120 ml (4 fl oz) olive oil
2 tablespoons lemon juice or
    white wine vinegar
120 ml (4 fl oz) soured cream
1 bunch radishes, quartered
1 head endive (frisé), broken
    into leaves
4 spring onions, cut lengthways
    and then into thirds
300 g (10 oz) fresh blackberries,
    rinsed

· Preheat oven to 200°C (400°F
  or gas 6).
· Rub chicken with salt and
  pepper. Place chicken in a
  roasting tin with the water.
  Roast for 1 hour, or until done.
  Allow to cool.

· Take meat from chicken by
  removing skin and separating
  all meat from bones, and set
  aside.
· In a bowl, whisk together egg
  yolk and mustard. Still whisking, gradually add olive oil and
  lemon juice or vinegar. Salt
  and pepper to taste.
· Combine the olive oil mixture
  with the soured cream. Toss
  chicken pieces with the soured
  cream dressing. Add radishes.
· Lay a bed of endive on each
  plate. Top with chicken and
  radish salad.
· Sprinkle cut spring onions over
  chicken. Arrange berries on
  plate.

Serves 7.
Preparation time: 2 hours.

38

PRAWN SALAD WITH REDCURRANTS

1 lemon, halved
10 black peppercorns
2 litres (3½ pints) cold water
125 g (4 oz) raw prawns
4 plum tomatoes
90 g (3 oz) redcurrants
salt and pepper
4 leaves cos lettuce

· Place halved lemon and peppercorns in 1 litre (1¾ pints)
  cold water. Heat to boiling;
  reduce heat and simmer for 5
  minutes. Place the prawns in
  the water and remove from
  heat. Allow to stand for 5
  minutes. Drain and let the
  prawns cool. Shell and devein
  prawns. Discard lemon and
  pepper.

· In a second pan, heat to
  boiling the remaining water.
  Place tomatoes in the water
  and blanch for about 3
  minutes.
· Transfer tomatoes into ice
  water. Skin the tomatoes, cut
  in half, remove seeds and dice.
  Mix with redcurrants in medium bowl. Add salt and
  pepper.
· Shred lettuce and arrange 2
  leaves on each plate.
· Place tomato-redcurrant mixture on top of the lettuce.
  Arrange the prawns on top of
  the mixture.

Serves 2.
Preparation time: 30 minutes.

CHICORY SALAD WITH BLACKBERRIES

juice of 1 lime
2 tablespoons balsamic vinegar
2 tablespoons sherry vinegar
2 tablespoons red wine vinegar
1 egg yolk
2 tablespoons Dijon mustard
2 tablespoons honey
1 tablespoon soy sauce
250 ml (8 fl oz) groundnut oil
2 tablespoons walnut oil
salt and pepper
2 heads chicory
30 g (1 oz) shelled walnuts,
  chopped
45 g (1½ oz) fresh blackberries

· Combine lime juice, vinegars, egg yolk, mustard, honey and soy sauce in a bowl. Whisk. Add oils, and salt and pepper to taste. Cover and refrigerate for about 2 hours.
· Separate the outer, larger leaves of the chicory and arrange on a plate. Just before serving, cut the remaining inner leaves into 5 mm (¼ inch) rings.
· Sprinkle walnuts and berries over the chicory leaves. Place chicory rings on top of salad.
· Drizzle about 2 tablespoons of the vinaigrette over salad. Refrigerate additional vinaigrette for later use.

Serves 2.
Preparation time: 2 hours, 15 minutes.

BITTER GREENS SALAD WITH STRAWBERRIES AND GOOSEBERRY VINAIGRETTE

2 tablespoons gooseberry
    preserve
2 tablespoons rice wine vinegar
1 teaspoon Dijon mustard
4 tablespoons safflower oil
4 tablespoons olive oil
2 tablespoons double cream
salt and pepper
10–12 small cauliflower florets
1 bunch watercress
1 bunch dandelion greens
125 g (4 oz) goat's cheese
75 g (2½ oz) strawberries

· Whisk together preserve and
  vinegar until smooth.

· Continue whisking, while
  slowly adding Dijon mustard
  and oils.
· Add cream, salt and pepper,
  whisking gently. Refrigerate,
  covered, for 1 hour.
· Drop cauliflower into 250 ml
  (8 fl oz) boiling water and boil
  for 1 minute. Remove florets
  from boiling water and refresh
  under cold water.
· Arrange greens on plates with
  cauliflower, goat's cheese and
  strawberries. Drizzle 2 tablespoons of dressing over each
  serving.

Serves 2.
Preparation time: 1 hour.

SMOKED TROUT AND RASPBERRY SALAD WITH LINGONBERRY DRESSING

250 ml (8 fl oz) crème fraîche
4 tablespoons lingonberry
    preserve
juice of 1 lemon
salt and pepper
2 bunches of rocket, washed
    thoroughly in cold water, and
    torn into bite-sized pieces
1 red onion, thinly sliced
1 whole smoked trout, about
    350 g (12 oz), picked off the
    bone and broken into bite-
    sized pieces
8 plum tomatoes, cut into
    quarters
125 g (4 oz) fresh raspberries

· In a small bowl, combine
  crème fraîche, preserve, lemon
  juice, salt and pepper.
· In medium bowl, toss rocket
  with red onion. Spread out on
  4 plates. Arrange trout pieces,
  tomato pieces and raspberries
  on top. Add dressing.

Serves 4.
Preparation time: 15 minutes.

FRUIT SALAD

2 medium-sized juicy oranges
2 limes
30 g (1 oz) raspberries
30 g (1 oz) golden raspberries
30 g (1 oz) strawberries
30 g (1 oz) blueberries
30 g (1 oz) blackberries
1 large papaya
2 kiwi fruit, peeled and sliced
20 g (⅔ oz) fresh coconut meat,
   shredded, or 25 g (scant 1 oz)
   desiccated coconut

· With a sharp paring knife,
  remove all skin from the
  oranges. Holding the oranges
  over a medium bowl to catch
  juices, cut along the membranes of the oranges so the
  segments fall into the bowl as
  well. Repeat the process for
  the limes.
· Add raspberries, strawberries,
  blueberries and blackberries.
  Cover and refrigerate for 2
  hours.
· Peel papaya, cut in half and
  remove the seeds. Cut each
  half into 1 cm (½ inch) slices
  and arrange on 4 plates with
  sliced kiwi fruit.
· Spoon berry and orange mixture, with juices, over papaya.
  Sprinkle with coconut.

Serves 4.
Preparation time: 15 minutes,
plus 2 hours chilling.

CRAB CAKES WITH BLACKBERRIES

750 ml–1 litre (1¼–1¾ pints)
   boiling water
125 g (4 oz) cornmeal
125 g (4 oz) unsalted butter
1 teaspoon salt
250 g (8 oz) fresh white
   crabmeat, cleaned
75 g (2½ oz) fresh blackberries
5 tablespoons soured cream
5 teaspoons black lumpfish
   caviar

· Add cornmeal, 60 g (2 oz)
butter and salt to the boiling
water and stir. Lower the heat
and continue stirring. When
cornmeal is smooth and has
absorbed all the water, set
aside and let cool.
· Combine cooked cornmeal
with crabmeat. Add blackberries. Form into 10 patties and
chill for 1 hour.
· In a large frying pan, melt
remaining butter over medium
to low heat. When butter begins to crackle (but not burn),
add the crab cakes. Cook on
each side until golden brown.
· Serve each portion of 2 crab
cakes with 1 tablespoon of
soured cream and 1 teaspoon
of caviar.

Serves 5.
Preparation time: 1½ hours.

BLACKENED TUNA
WITH STRAWBERRIES

60 g (2 oz) unsalted butter
5–6 large strawberries, hulled
   and cut into thirds
½ teaspoon ground cumin
½ teaspoon ground cinnamon
½ teaspoon ground marjoram
½ teaspoon ground cayenne
   pepper
salt and pepper
2 × 250 g (8 oz) tuna steaks
4 tablespoons groundnut oil

· In small frying pan over low
heat, melt the butter and add
strawberries. Sauté strawberries
for 3 minutes, until soft. Set
aside.

· Mix together cumin, cinnamon, marjoram, cayenne
pepper, salt and pepper.
Season tuna generously
with mixture.
· In small cast-iron frying pan,
heat groundnut oil over high
heat. Sear fish until black,
about 3–4 minutes. Turn over
and blacken other side, another 2–3 minutes. (This will
produce a lot of smoke.)
· Garnish tuna with strawberries
and serve.

Serves 2.
Preparation time: 15 minutes.

STUFFED LOBSTER WITH CRANBERRIES

30 g (1 oz) unsalted butter
2 tablespoons plain flour
250 ml (8 fl oz) single cream
50 g (scant 2 oz) cranberries
60 g (2 oz) canned sweet-corn,
    drained, or 45 g (1½ oz) fresh
    sweet-corn kernels
¼ red pepper, finely chopped
1 mild green chilli, seeded and
    finely chopped
salt and pepper
1 × 750 g (1½ lb) live lobster

· In a frying pan over medium
  heat, melt butter and add the
  flour. Whisk together for 4–5
  minutes to form a roux. The
  roux will be extremely hot.
· Using whisk, add cream
  slowly. Set aside.
· In a saucepan, bring 250 ml (8
  fl oz) of water to the boil.
  Cook cranberries for about 1
  minute, or until the cranberries
  begin to split. Drain cranberries and discard cooking liquid.
· Add sweet-corn, red pepper,
  chilli and cranberries to the
  cream mixture. Add salt and
  pepper. Set aside.
· In a large pan bring 4 litres (7
  pints) of water to the boil.
  Lower to a simmer. Put the
  lobster in the pan by holding
  the body, claws facing down.
  Cover and cook for 6 minutes.

· Split the lobster in half lengthways with a large, heavy knife.
  To do this, cut from the base
  of the head towards the tail,
  with shell side up. Turn lobster
  around and split head. With a
  fork, remove meat from the
  tail and chop coarsely. Combine with the sweet-corn and
  pepper mixture. Stuff mixture
  back into the tail shell. (Can be
  refrigerated, covered with cling
  film, for up to 2 days.)
· Preheat oven to 220°C (425°F
  or gas 7). Place lobster in
  baking dish. Bake lobster for
  8–10 minutes.

Serves 2.
Preparation time: 1 hour.

BARBECUED SWORDFISH WITH REDCURRANT BUTTER

120 ml (4 fl oz) water
3 tablespoons fresh redcurrants
60 g (2 oz) unsalted butter,
    softened to room temperature
salt and pepper
2 × 250 g (8 oz) pieces
    swordfish or tuna
1 tablespoon olive oil

· In a 1 litre saucepan, bring to a
  simmer the water. Add the
  redcurrants and poach for 1
  minute. Drain the redcurrants
  and allow to cool. Combine
  redcurrants, butter, and salt
  and pepper.

· Form the redcurrant butter
  into a 12.5 cm (5 inch) log.
  Place it in the butter wrapper,
  cling film, or greaseproof paper and refrigerate for 1 hour.
· Prepare and heat barbecue, or
  preheat grill to high.
· Season swordfish with salt and
  pepper. Rub with olive oil.
  Barbecue or grill both sides of
  swordfish for 3–4 minutes
  each, until tender to the touch.
· Garnish each piece of fish with
  a slice of redcurrant butter.

Serves 2.
Preparation time: 1 hour and 15
minutes.

STEAMED PRAWNS WITH CRANBERRY COULIS

4 tablespoons Cranberry
   Gazpacho (see page 30)
425 ml (14 fl oz) water
100 g (3½ oz) basmati rice
salt and pepper
12 large raw prawns
4 tablespoons very finely
   chopped parsley

· Prepare Cranberry Gazpacho
  and set aside.
· In a small saucepan, bring to
  the boil 175 ml (6 fl oz) water.
  Add the rice and lower the
  heat. Stir, while adding salt
  and pepper. Cover and cook
  for 12–15 minutes, until all the
  liquid is absorbed. Set aside.
· In a small saucepan on medium heat, heat the Cranberry
Gazpacho. Add 2 tablespoons
of water and cook until the
water is evaporated. Cover. Set
aside.
· In a deep saucepan, bring to
  the boil 1 cup of water. Place
  the prawns in a strainer and
  place the strainer in the saucepan. Cover and cook for about
  3–4 minutes, or until prawns
  are firm and opaque. Drain
  and set aside.
· Toss parsley with rice, and
  arrange on plates.
· Place Cranberry Gazpacho on
  the rice.
· Arrange prawns on plates.

Serves 2.
Preparation time: 1 hour, includ-
ing preparation of gazpacho.

SQUID INK FETTUCINE WITH BLACKBERRY CREAM SAUCE

250 ml (8 fl oz) boiling water
4 spears asparagus, trimmed
    and cut in 5 cm (2 inch) long
    pieces
30 g (1 oz) unsalted butter
3 large shallots, peeled and
    sliced into rings
5½ tablespoons dry white wine
175 ml (6 fl oz) double cream
3 plum tomatoes, cut into
    quarters
150 g (5 oz) fresh blackberries
salt and pepper to taste
2 litres (3½ pints) water
300 g (10 oz) fresh squid ink
    fettucine, or white or green
    tagliatelle

· Blanch asparagus in boiling
  water for 1 minute. Drain and
  refresh under cold water until
  cold throughout. Set aside.
· In a large frying pan, melt
  butter and add shallots. Cook
  until translucent.
· Add wine and bring to the
  boil. Allow to reduce by half.
  Add the double cream and
  reduce mixture by half. Lower
  the heat.
· Add the tomatoes, asparagus,
  blackberries, salt and pepper.
· Heat water, lightly salted, to
  boiling in a large pan. Cook
  fettucine for 3 minutes, or
  until done. Drain and mix the
  pasta with the sauce in medium bowl.

Serves 2.
Preparation time: 15 minutes.

PAN-FRIED FISH WITH BLUEBERRY BUTTER SAUCE

2 × 250 g (8 oz) sea bass fillets
salt and pepper
4 tablespoons plain flour
2 tablespoons groundnut oil
5½ tablespoons blueberry
    vinegar
4 tablespoons double cream
60 g (2 oz) unsalted butter,
    softened

· Preheat oven to 220°C (425°F
  or gas 7).
· Season fish fillets with salt and
  pepper. Dust lightly with flour.
  Set aside.
· In a large frying pan, heat oil
  until it smokes. Place fish in
pan and brown on one side.
Turn over and remove from
pan. Place in baking tin and
cook in oven for about 6
minutes.
· Remove fish from oven and
  return to frying pan. Raise to
  high heat.
· Add vinegar and allow liquid
  to reduce almost completely.
  Add double cream and bring
  to the boil.
· After cream has thickened
  gradually add the butter. Add
  salt and pepper.
· Place fish on plates and spoon
  sauce on top.

Serves 2.
Preparation time: 15 minutes.

PORK RIBS WITH RASPBERRY BARBECUE SAUCE

2 racks of pork spareribs (about
    12 bones each), skin peeled
    off backs
salt and pepper
350 ml (12 fl oz) water
350 g (12 oz) raspberry jam
250 ml (8 fl oz) tomato ketchup
1 onion, finely chopped
½ teaspoon cayenne pepper

· Preheat oven to 130°C (250°F
  or gas ½).
· Tie the two racks together
  with non-coated string, so the
  curves of the bone face one
  another. Season with salt and
  pepper.

· Stand ribs in a roasting tin.
  Add the water. Cover with
  kitchen foil.
· Roast for 2 hours, until your
  fingers touch through the meat
  when you pinch between two
  bones. Set aside.
· In a frying pan over low heat,
  combine jam, ketchup,
  chopped onion and cayenne
  pepper. Simmer for 5 minutes.
  Add salt and pepper to taste.
  Thin with water if sauce becomes too thick.
· Cut rib racks in half, so there
  are about 5–6 bones per section. Cover with barbecue
  sauce and serve.

Serves 4–6.
Preparation time: 3 hours.

ROAST LAMB WITH LINGONBERRY SAUCE

1 × 175–250 g (6–8 oz) boned
    loin of lamb
salt and pepper
2 cloves garlic, finely chopped
1 slice of bread, any type
4 tablespoons sherry, brandy or
    red wine
4 tablespoons chicken stock (see
    page 28)
30 g (1 oz) lingonberries, fresh
    or in syrup
15 g (½ oz) unsalted butter

· Preheat oven to 230°C (450°F
  or gas 8).
· Remove all fat from meat.
  With a sharp knife cut off the
  silverskin, or shiny outer skin
  from the meat. Season with
  salt and pepper. In a very hot,
  ovenproof frying pan, briefly
  sear both sides of the loin,
  until golden brown, over high
  heat on stove.

· Remove from heat and rub
  garlic on both sides.
· Place the slice of bread in the
  centre of the pan and top with
  the lamb. This elevation helps
  the meat to cook evenly. Roast
  for 5–10 minutes, until cooked
  to taste. The handle of the pan
  will be very hot.
· Slice lamb on a slant and
  arrange on plate.
· Return pan to top of stove.
  Over medium high heat, pour
  sherry into pan. Momentary
  flames will rise. Reduce sherry
  somewhat, and add chicken
  stock.
· Bring stock to the boil and
  allow to reduce for 1 minute.
  Add the lingonberries (drain if
  in syrup) and butter. Swirl pan
  until the butter melts evenly.
  Add salt and pepper to taste.
  Pour sauce over sliced lamb.

Serves 2.
Preparation time: 30 minutes.

BRAISED PORK CHOP WITH BLUEBERRY CREAM SAUCE

2 × 175–250 g (6–8 oz) pork
    chops
salt and pepper
120 ml (4 fl oz) sherry
35 g (1¼ oz) dried blueberries
120 ml (4 fl oz) double cream
Note: dried blackcurrants may
    be substituted for dried
    blueberries

· Preheat oven to 200°C (400°F
  or gas 6).
· Season pork chops with salt
  and pepper.
· In a hot ovenproof frying pan,
  sear both sides of pork chops
  over high heat on stove.

· Pour sherry around sides of
  pan. Momentary flames will
  rise. When flames subside, add
  blueberries.
· Cover entire pan with kitchen
  foil, and put in the oven to
  cook for 15 minutes, until the
  chops are firm to the touch.
· Set the pork chops aside and
  return pan to a high heat.
  Handle will be extremely hot.
· Reduce liquid by half and add
  cream. Bring to the boil and
  cook for about 2 minutes, until
  cream thickens. Add salt and
  pepper to taste.
· Pour sauce over pork chops
  and serve.

Serves 2.
Preparation time: 30 minutes.

GRILLED CHICKEN BREAST WITH GOLDEN RASPBERRY CAKES

2 cloves garlic, finely chopped
120 ml (4 fl oz) blueberry
    vinegar
juice of 1 lime
350 ml (12 fl oz) virgin olive oil
1 tablespoon whole black
    peppercorns, crushed
4 boneless chicken breasts,
    pounded thin
1 large yellow or green courgette
1 egg
15 g (½ oz) fresh breadcrumbs
60 g (2 oz) fresh golden
    raspberries
salt and pepper

· In a large bowl, combine the
  garlic, blueberry vinegar, lime
  juice, 250 ml (8 fl oz) olive oil
  and crushed black peppercorns. Place the chicken in the
  marinade and set aside for 1
  hour.
· Grate the courgette into a
  large mixing bowl. Add the
  egg, breadcrumbs, golden
  raspberries, salt and pepper.
  Form 4 patties and refrigerate
  for 1 hour.
· Prepare and heat barbecue, or
  preheat grill to high. With
  skin side up, place chicken on
  the hottest part of the barbecue grid, or under the grill.
  Cook, turning every 1 or 2
  minutes until done.
· In a large frying pan heat
  remaining oil until it smokes.
  Place the cakes in the pan,
  lower heat and cook on both
  sides until golden brown.
· Serve with Rosehip
  Mayonnaise.

Serves 2.
Preparation time: 2 hours.

ROSEHIP MAYONNAISE

2 egg yolks
1 tablespoon Dijon mustard
1 tablespoon lemon juice
500 ml (16 fl oz) olive oil
salt and pepper
2 tablespoons rosehip syrup

· Combine egg yolks, mustard
  and lemon juice.
· Whisk in the olive oil drop by
  drop. Add salt and pepper.
  When mixture is firm, fold in
  rosehip syrup.

Makes 600 ml (1 pint)
mayonnaise.
Preparation time: 10 minutes.

CHICKEN-KUMQUAT SKEWERS WITH SPICY CRANBERRY KETCHUP

10 × 15 cm (6 inch) bamboo
  skewers
5 boneless chicken breasts
20 kumquats, left whole
125 g (4 oz) fresh cranberries
125 g (4 oz) tomato purée
120 ml (4 fl oz) red wine vinegar
4 mild green chillies, seeded and
  finely chopped
20 shakes Tabasco sauce
50 g (scant 2 oz) caster sugar
salt and pepper
4 tablespoons vegetable oil

· Soak bamboo skewers in water
  for 30 minutes to prevent
  burning them during cooking.
· Cut each chicken breast into
  6 equal pieces.
· On each skewer alternate 3
  pieces of chicken with 2
  kumquats.

· Bring to the boil a large pan of
  water. Cook cranberries for
  about 2 minutes, until berries
  begin to split. Drain.
· Place cranberries, tomato
  purée, vinegar, chillies, Tabasco sauce, sugar, salt and
  pepper in a food processor.
  Purée until smooth. Push
  through a fine-mesh sieve.
· Prepare and heat barbecue, or
  preheat grill to high.
· Brush each skewer lightly with
  vegetable oil. Salt and pepper
  to taste.
· Place on the barbecue grid, or
  under the grill and cook until
  chicken is cooked throughout,
  turning often. Serve each
  skewer with 2 tablespoons
  cranberry ketchup.

Makes 10 skewers.
Preparation time: 45 minutes.

ROAST DUCK BREAST
WITH PHYSALIS

2 tablespoons groundnut oil
2 medium-sized duck breasts
4 tablespoons white zinfandel,
    or other blush or light rosé
    wine
4 tablespoons chicken stock (see
    page 28)
30 g (1 oz) husked physalis
    (Cape gooseberries)
15 g (½ oz) cold unsalted butter
salt and pepper

· Preheat oven to 230°C (450°F
  or gas 8).
· In a heavy ovenproof frying
  pan, heat oil until smoking.
  Place duck in pan, skin side
  down. Cook for about 3 minutes over high heat on stove.
Turn duck over and place pan
into the oven. Roast for 8
minutes, until firm to the
touch, with slight resistance.
Slice the breasts and arrange
on a plate. Cover and set
aside.
· Return pan to the stove. Over
  a high heat, add the wine.
  Bring to the boil and allow to
  reduce by about half. Add
  chicken stock and physalis.
  Bring to the boil and allow
  liquid to reduce. Add butter
  and salt and pepper. Pour
  sauce over sliced duck breasts.

Serves 2.
Preparation time: 25 minutes.

HOLIDAY TURKEY WITH CRANBERRY SAUCE

1 × 3 kg (6 pound) turkey with
   giblets
salt and pepper
350 ml (12 fl oz) water
2 Granny Smith apples
2 sprigs fresh mint
1 stick cinnamon
3–4 whole cloves
125 g (4 oz) cranberries
50 g (scant 2 oz) caster sugar or
   to taste
30 g (1 oz) unsalted butter
2 tablespoons plain flour

· Preheat oven to 190°C (375°F
  or gas 5).
· Rinse turkey thoroughly with
  water. Rub evenly with salt
  and pepper. Open bag of
  giblets and rinse giblets.
· Place turkey in a 5 cm (2 inch)
  deep roasting tin with the
  water. Add giblets to water
  and roast for about 1½ hours
  or until juices run clear from
  the joints. Baste at 15 minute
  intervals. Add more water if
  necessary.
· Peel and core apples, reserving
  skins. In muslin tie skins,
cores, mint, cinnamon and
cloves. Place apples, cranberries and *bouquet garni* of skins
and spices in a large saucepan
with enough cold water to
cover ingredients.
· Cook over a moderately high
  heat for 1 hour. Stir often with
  a wooden spoon and add more
  water, if necessary. Lower the
  heat if necessary. When water
  is replenished, use cold water
  and bring liquid back to the
  boil; then lower to a simmer.
  This process will soften the
  apples and cranberries and
  make the sauce smoother.
· Remove *bouquet garni*, add
  sugar to taste and set aside.
· When turkey is cooked, set it
  aside for 10 minutes. Strain the
  roasting juices and set aside.
· To make gravy, melt the butter
  in a frying pan and add the
  flour. Whisk together to form
  a roux. Add the juices from
  the turkey and water, if necessary. Add salt and pepper.
· Serve turkey with gravy, warm,
  and cranberry sauce.

Serves 4.
Preparation time: 2 hours.

CHAPTER FOUR · DESSERTS

LINZER BISCUITS

200 g (7 oz) caster sugar
265 g (8½ oz) unsalted butter
½ teaspoon salt
1 teaspoon vanilla essence
280 g (10 oz) plain flour
325 g (11 oz) raspberry jam
60 g (2 oz) icing sugar

· Mix caster sugar, 250 g (8 oz) butter, salt and vanilla essence until smooth. Add flour. Mix until incorporated and dough forms a ball.
· Form into a log and refrigerate for 1 hour.
· Preheat oven to 180°C (350°F or gas 4).
· Cut log into 20 equal pieces. Roll each piece to about 5 mm (¼ inch) thickness.
· With a 10 cm (4 inch) fluted round cutter, press biscuits out of the rolled dough. With a 1 cm (½ inch) round cutter, press a hole in the centre of half the biscuits.
· Butter a large baking sheet with remaining butter and place biscuits at 2.5 cm (1 inch) intervals. Bake for 8–10 minutes, until biscuits turn golden brown. Remove from baking sheet and cool.
· Spread jam on the biscuits without centre holes.
· Top with the biscuits with centre holes.
· Place icing sugar in a sieve and dust over the biscuits.

Makes 10 biscuits.
Preparation time: 1½ hours.

RASPBERRY AND BLUEBERRY TARTLETS WITH LEMON CREAM

LEMON CREAM

grated zest and juice of
   3 lemons
3 egg yolks
3 tablespoons caster sugar
120 ml (4 fl oz) double cream
75 g (2½ oz) blueberries
60 g (2 oz) raspberries

TARTLET SHELLS

140 g (5 oz) plain flour
125 g (4 oz) cold unsalted butter,
   cut into small pieces
½ teaspoon salt
2 tablespoons caster sugar

LEMON CREAM:

· In a glass or stainless steel
  bowl, combine lemon zest,
  lemon juice, egg yolks and
  sugar. Place in a double boiler
  and stir until the mixture
  firms. Refrigerate for 3 hours.
  Mixture will continue to firm
  when cooled.
· While mixture is in refrigerator, prepare tartlet shells.

TARTLET SHELLS:

· In a large bowl mix flour,
  butter, salt and sugar with
  fingertips.
· Add a few tablespoons of cold
  water to bind the dough.
· Divide the dough in quarters,
  and refrigerate for 2 hours.
· Preheat oven to 180°C (350°F
  or gas 4).
· On a clean, flat surface, roll
  out dough and press into four
  10 cm (4 inch) tartlet tins.
  Bake blind for about 25 minutes, until golden brown. Allow to cool.
· While tartlet shells cool, remove lemon mixture from refrigerator and proceed with
  lemon cream.

· In a clean bowl, whip the
  cream until thick.
· Mix some of the whipped
  cream with the lemon mixture;
  then fold that mixture into the
  rest of the whipped cream.
  Spread into tartlet shells.
· Arrange blueberries and raspberries on top of the lemon
  cream.

Serves 4.
Preparation time: 3½ hours.

BLUEBERRY PIE

250 g (8 oz) cold unsalted
   butter, cut into small pieces
280 g (10 oz) plain flour
150 g (5 oz) caster sugar
2 teaspoons salt
4–5 tablespoons ice water
300 g (10 oz) fresh blueberries
1 egg
2 tablespoons water

· Mix butter, flour, 50 g (scant 2
  oz) sugar and 1 teaspoon salt
  with fork or fingers until mixture has the consistency of
  coarse cornmeal. Add ice
  water, 1 tablespoon at a time,
  until dough binds.
· Divide the dough in half, wrap
  in plastic and refrigerate for
  about 2 hours.
· Preheat oven to 180°C (350°F
  or gas 4).

· On a clean, dry surface, sprinkle some flour and roll out one
  of the dough pieces. Press into
  a 20 cm (8 inch) pie plate or
  flan tin.
· In a medium bowl, toss blueberries with remaining sugar
  and 1 teaspoon salt. Turn blueberries into pastry shell.
· Roll out remaining dough, and
  cut into 2 cm (¾ inch) wide
  strips. Arrange on top of pie in
  a criss-cross pattern. Crimp
  edges.
· Beat the egg with the water
  and brush over the pastry
  strips and edge of the shell.
· Bake for 45–50 minutes, or
  until golden brown.

Serves 6.
Preparation time: 3 hours.

BLACKBERRY CUSTARD

1 teaspoon unsalted butter
100 g (3½ oz) caster sugar
2 egg yolks
500 ml (16 fl oz) double cream
75 g (2½ oz) fresh blackberries

· Preheat oven to 180°C (350°F
  or gas 4).
· Grease four 175 ml (6 fl oz)
  ramekins or soufflé dishes with
  the butter and coat with 2
  tablespoons sugar.
· Combine egg yolks and 4
  tablespoons sugar. Beat until
  mixture turns light yellow.
  Add cream. Skim off surface
  foam. Add blackberries, reserving 2 or 3 berries.

· Mash reserved berries with a
  fork. Add remaining 2 tablespoons sugar and a few drops
  of water. Set aside.
· Pour egg mixture into the
  ramekins. Place the ramekins
  in a roasting tin filled with
  enough water to come halfway
  up the sides of the ramekins.
· Bake for 45 minutes or until
  firm. Remove from tin and
  allow to cool, about 1 hour.
  Turn out upside down on to
  plate and cover with mashed
  berry sauce.

Serves 4.
Preparation time: 2 hours.

CHOCOLATE CAKE WITH FRAMBOISE-SOAKED RASPBERRIES

180 g (6 oz) fresh raspberries
120 ml (4 fl oz) framboise
350 g (12 oz) plain chocolate
350 g (12 oz) unsalted butter
7 tablespoons caster sugar
125 g (4 oz) shelled walnuts
6 eggs
2 tablespoons cornflour,
    dissolved in 2 tablespoons
    framboise

· Preheat oven to 180°C (350°F or gas 4).
· Soak 120 g (4 oz) raspberries in framboise for 2 hours.
· In top of double boiler combine chocolate, butter and 5 tablespoons sugar, and melt. Allow to cool.
· In a blender, grind walnuts into a fine powder. Transfer to a medium bowl and add eggs, soaked raspberries and cornflour.
· Combine walnut mixture with cooled chocolate mixture, and pour into a 30 cm (12 inch) springform cake tin.
· Bake for about 40 minutes, until firm to the touch. While cake is baking, prepare raspberry sauce.
· In a medium saucepan place remaining raspberries, 2 tablespoons sugar and 1 tablespoon of water. Over a low heat, cook for 10 minutes, stirring occasionally. Sieve and cool. (Sauce can be refrigerated overnight.)
· Refrigerate cake overnight to set. Unmould and serve with sauce.

Serves 12.
Preparation time: 3 hours, plus overnight chilling.

PISTACHIO AND ORANGE SOUFFLÉ WITH HOT BLUEBERRY SAUCE

15 g (½ oz) unsalted butter
2 tablespoons finely chopped
  pistachios
7 tablespoons caster sugar
75 g (2½ oz) fresh blueberries
2 eggs, separated
grated zest of 1 orange
2 teaspoons Grand Marnier, or
  other orange-flavoured
  liqueur

· Preheat oven to 180°C (350°F
  or gas 4).
· Butter two 175 g (6 fl oz)
  soufflé dishes.
· Combine the chopped
  pistachios with 2 tablespoons
  of sugar and dust into soufflé
  dishes. Chill while continuing
  recipe.
· In a medium pan over a low
  heat, cook the blueberries with
  3 tablespoons sugar and a few
drops of water. Add more
water if necessary. Cook until
blueberries split. Lower heat to
keep blueberries warm.
· Combine egg yolks, orange
  zest, Grand Marnier and remaining sugar.
· In deep, narrow bowl, whisk
  egg whites until stiff peaks
  form. Fold some of the egg
  whites into the yolk mixture;
  then fold the egg yolk mixture
  into the remaining egg whites.
· Using a rubber spatula, fill the
  2 dishes with the mixture.
  Place the dishes in a roasting
  tin filled with enough water to
  reach halfway up the sides of
  the dishes. Bake for 10 minutes, until the soufflé rises
  above the edge of the dish.
· Spoon the blueberry sauce on
  top of the soufflé and serve
  immediately.

Serves 2.
Preparation time: 25 minutes.

92

HAZELNUT CHEESECAKE WITH BLACKBERRIES

150 g (5 oz) blackberries
300 g (10 oz) caster sugar
75 g (2½ oz) shelled hazelnuts
125 g (4 oz) cream cheese
120 ml (4 fl oz) soured cream
125 g (4 oz) ricotta cheese
2 eggs
pinch of salt
½ teaspoon vanilla essence
125 g (4 oz) unsalted butter
140 g (5 oz) plain flour

· Preheat oven to 180°C (350°F or gas 4).
· In medium bowl, combine blackberries with 100 g (3½ oz) sugar. Cover and refrigerate for 1 hour.
· Roast hazelnuts in a shallow tin for 5 minutes. Cool and chop coarsely.
· In clean bowl, combine 100 g (3½ oz) sugar, cream cheese, soured cream, ricotta cheese, eggs, salt and vanilla essence. Set aside.
· In another bowl, cream remaining sugar with butter. Add flour and a couple of drops of water. Mix until the dough binds. Add roasted hazelnuts.
· Roll out dough and press into a 22.5 cm (9 inch) round cake tin. Fill with cream cheese mixture.
· Bake for 1 hour, until the cake is firm to the touch.
· Chill for 2 hours.
· Cover individual slices with blackberries and syrup.

Serves 6.
Preparation time: 4 hours.

RASPBERRY FOOL

125 g (4 oz) fresh raspberries
2 egg yolks
2 tablespoons caster sugar
250 ml (8 fl oz) double cream
grated zest of 1 lime

· Sieve the raspberries and discard the seeds. Add the egg yolks and sugar to the raspberry purée.
· Place the mixture in a double boiler, and stir slowly with a rubber spatula for 10 minutes, until it begins to firm. Refrigerate for 1 hour. The mixture will become firmer as it chills.
· In a tall, narrow bowl, whip cream till stiff peaks form. Fold a bit of whipped cream into the raspberry mixture. Fold the raspberry mixture into the remaining whipped cream. Sprinkle lime zest on top and serve.

Serves 4.
Preparation time: 1½ hours.

COEURS À LA CRÈME

125 g (4 oz) cream cheese,
    softened
1 teaspoon vanilla essence
2–3 tablespoons icing sugar
120 ml (4 fl oz) double cream
60 g (2 oz) fresh raspberries
2 tablespoons caster sugar

· In a medium bowl, blend
  cream cheese, vanilla essence
  and icing sugar until creamy.
· In a deep, narrow bowl, whip
  double cream until firm.
· Mix some of the whipped
  cream with the cream cheese
  mixture; then fold the cream
  cheese mixture into the remaining whipped cream.
· Line 2 coeurs à la crème
  moulds* with damp muslin.
  Fill the lined moulds with the
cream cheese mixture. Refrigerate the moulds overnight on
a plate to catch whey, or
drippings.
· In a medium saucepan place
  all but 6 to 8 of the raspberries, the caster sugar and 1
  tablespoon of water. Over a
  low heat, cook for 10 minutes.
  Stir occasionally. Add more
  water if necessary. Sieve and
  cool.
· Unmould coeurs à la crème,
  and serve with remaining
  raspberries and sauce.

Serves 2.
Preparation time: 15 minutes,
plus overnight chilling.

*These moulds come in two
sizes—large and small—and
are available at speciality kitch-
enware shops.

GÉNOISE WITH LINGONBERRY BUTTER CREAM

GÉNOISE

1 teaspoon butter
140 g (5 oz) plain flour
6 eggs
150 g (5 oz) caster sugar
pinch of salt
60 g (2 oz) unsalted butter,
    melted and cooled

LINGONBERRY BUTTER CREAM

4 egg yolks
60 g (2 oz) sugar
250 g (8 oz) unsalted butter,
    softened
350 g (12 oz) lingonberry
    preserve
120 ml (4 fl oz) double cream

GÉNOISE:

· Preheat oven to 180°C (350°F
  or gas 4).
· Butter two 22.5 cm (9 inch)
  round cake tins with ½ teaspoon butter each. Sprinkle
  each with 2 tablespoons of
  flour. Discard excess flour.
  Refrigerate.
· In a bowl, beat eggs and sugar
  until very firm and pale (over
  hot water if not using electric
  mixer).
· Sift remaining flour and salt
  into egg and sugar mixture.

Fold until incorporated.
· Add melted butter and continue folding.
· Pour mixture into cake tins.
  Tap the tins lightly against
  work surface to eliminate large
  air pockets. Do not bang too
  hard or the mixture will
  deflate.
· Bake for 20–25 minutes, or
  until edges shrink away from
  the tin and a skewer inserted
  in the centre comes out clean.
· Allow to cool. Cut each cake in
  half horizontally.

LINGONBERRY BUTTER CREAM:

· In a bowl, beat egg yolks and
  icing sugar until the mixture
  becomes a light yellow colour.
· Add the softened butter gradually until it is evenly incorporated. Refrigerate for 1 hour.
· Add the preserve to the butter
  cream. Refrigerate for 1 hour.
· In a deep, narrow bowl, whip
  the double cream until stiff.
· Spread the butter cream evenly
  over each cake half. Spread the
  whipped cream over all but
  one of the halves, on top of
  the butter cream. The layer
  without whipped cream will be
  the top layer. Assemble cake.

Serves 6.
Preparation time: 2½ hours.

BLUEBERRY SORBET

1 litre (1¾ pints) lemon-lime
   flavoured, carbonated drink
150 g (5 oz) fresh blueberries

· Pour drink into a 5 cm (2 inch)
  deep flat pan. Place, uncovered, in the freezer. Freeze
  until solid.
· Remove from freezer and
  scrape frozen drink with the
  dull edge of a knife into a
  medium-sized bowl. Add blueberries to the slush.
· Cover the mixture and return
  to freezer.
· Freeze until firm.

Serves 10.
Preparation time: 3 hours.

STRAWBERRY ICE CREAM

5 egg yolks
1 litre (1¾ pints) double cream
200 g (7 oz) caster sugar
1–1½ tablespoons strawberry-
   flavoured liqueur
75 g (2½ oz) fresh strawberries

· Combine all ingredients.
· Follow instructions for your
  ice-cream machine. Use a machine with a 1.5 litre (2½ pint)
  capacity.
· Cover and store in freezer.

Serves 10.
Preparation time: 45 minutes.

CHOCOLATE-DIPPED STRAWBERRIES

125 g (4 oz) plain chocolate
6 strawberries

· Melt the chocolate in a double
  boiler.
· Holding the strawberries by
  the stalk, dip each one in the
  melted chocolate until evenly
  covered. Place on greaseproof
  paper and refrigerate.

Serves 2.
Preparation time: 20 minutes.

SUMMER PUDDING

200–300 g (8–10 oz) fresh
    berries (raspberries,
    blackberries, strawberries and
    blackcurrants all work well
    combined or alone)
100 g (3½ oz) caster sugar
500 ml (16 fl oz) double cream
6 slices white bread, crusts
    trimmed off

· Toss the berries with half of
  the sugar, and set aside for 1
  hour. Berries will give off juice.
· In a deep, narrow bowl, whip
  the cream to stiff peaks with
  the remaining sugar. Cover
  and refrigerate.
· Cut the bread into 2.5 cm (1
  inch) squares.

· In 2 goblets or small dessert
  bowls, place several berries
  along with 1 tablespoon of
  juice per serving.
· Spread 2 tablespoons of
  whipped cream on top of the
  berries.
· Cover the whipped cream with
  a layer of bread pieces. Repeat
  the procedure, layering berries
  with juice, whipped cream and
  bread pieces until the bowls
  are filled. Cover and refrigerate overnight.
· Top with the remaining
  whipped cream and a few
  berries as garnish.

Serves 2.
Preparation time: 1 hour, plus
overnight chilling.

CRANBERRY GINGER TEA

500 ml (16 fl oz) boiling water
75 g (2½ oz) fresh root ginger,
  thinly sliced
50 g (scant 2 oz) fresh
  cranberries, rinsed
pinch nutmeg
120 ml (4 fl oz) cranberry juice
2 sprigs of mint

· In a medium-sized bowl, pour
  boiling water over ginger and
  cranberries. Cover and allow to
  stand for 20 minutes. Strain,
  add nutmeg and cranberry
  juice and stir.
· Serve warm or chilled over ice
  cubes. Garnish with mint.

Serves 2.
Preparation time: 25 minutes.

BLUEBERRY YOGURT SHAKE

500 ml (16 fl oz) plain yogurt
120 ml (4 fl oz) orange juice,
  freshly squeezed
150 g (5 oz) fresh blueberries,
  rinsed
1 banana, very ripe

· Combine all ingredients in a
  blender. Blend on medium
  speed until smooth and frothy.
· Pour into glasses and serve.

Serves 4.
Preparation time: 3 minutes.

NUTTY RASPBERRY

1½ tablespoons hazelnut-
    flavoured liqueur
1½ tablespoons raspberry-
    flavoured brandy
1½ tablespoons double cream
    (optional)

· Combine in a cocktail glass,
  over ice.
· If using cream, combine in a
  shaker. Shake and pour into a
  glass, over ice.

Serves 2.
Preparation time: 1 minute.

FRAMBOISE
AND CHAMPAGNE

2 tablespoons framboise, or
    raspberry-flavoured brandy
120 ml (4 fl oz) champagne,
    chilled

· Pour framboise into champagne glasses. Add
  champagne.

Serves 2.
Preparation time: 1 minute.

BERRY ICE CUBES

12 blueberries
12 raspberries

· Fill 2 ice cube trays with 1 or 2
  berries in each section. Cover
  with warm water and freeze
  overnight.

Makes 20 ice cubes, with 10-
cube trays.
Preparation time: 1 minute,
plus overnight freezing.

STRAWBERRY MARGARITA

450 g (15 oz) fresh strawberries,
  hulled
5–6 ice cubes, crushed
juice of 1 lime
3 tablespoons golden tequila

· In a blender, on low speed,
  combine all ingredients.

Serves 2.
Preparation time: 1 minute.

STRAWBERRY DAIQUIRI

150 g (5 oz) fresh strawberries,
  hulled
5–6 ice cubes, crushed
juice of 1 lime
3 tablespoons light rum

· In a blender, on low speed,
  combine all ingredients.

Serves 2.
Preparation time: 1 minute.

RASPBERRY PUNCH

1 litre (1¾ pints) ginger ale
120 ml (4 fl oz) golden rum
120 ml (4 fl oz) raspberry-
    flavoured brandy
juice of 1 lime

· Combine ingredients, propor-
  tionately to taste.

Serves 10.
Preparation time: 5 minutes.

RASPBERRY EGGNOG

1 litre (1¾ pints) double cream
1 litre (1¾ pints) milk
4 eggs
pinch of nutmeg
500 ml (16 fl oz) raspberry-
    flavoured brandy
200 g (7 oz) caster sugar
1 litre (2 pints) vanilla ice cream

· Combine ingredients, propor-
  tionately to taste.

Serves 15.
Preparation time: 5 minutes.

*For both recipes, the amounts
and proportions ought to be
determined by personal taste.
Begin with all ingredients listed,
and taste as you gradually add
each ingredient.

RECIPE LIST

RECIPE LIST BY BERRY